BAD HABIT
Rabbit

BY Carli Valentine

Text and Illustration Copyright © 2022 Carli Valentine
Book design by Carli Valentine

Published in 2022 by Design By Valentine LLC, in North Ogden, UT, USA. All rights reserved. No part of this book may be reproduced or used in any manner without written permission of the copyright owner except for the use of quotations in a book review. For more information, address: carliavalentine@gmail.com

First paperback edition March 2022

Printed and bound in the United States

Library of Congress Control Number:
2022904086

Book authored and illustrated by Carli Valentine

ISBN (Paperback)- 978-1-957505-05-3
ISBN (Hardcover)- 978-1-957505-04-6

Visit www.carlivalentine.com
www.instagram.com/carlivalentineauthor
www.facebook.com/Carli-Valentine-Childrens-Book-AuthorIllustrator-102280112241008/
www.amazon.com/Carli-Valentine/e/B09JL7V5NB/

To Keaton, my honey bunny.
Thank you for all your
love and support.

-C.V.

Did you ever wonder how an
Easter Bunny is chosen to hold that legendary title?

Well it all starts out at Bunny Hospital
where promising bunnies are
hand selected by the E.B.P. (Easter Bunny Pickers).

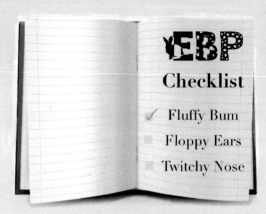

EBP

Checklist

✓ Fluffy Bum

☐ Floppy Ears

☐ Twitchy Nose

How do they pick the promising candidates, you ask? They have a checklist of things they look for with each rabbit that is born.

But that is a story for another time. Today I am going to focus on a special little rabbit named Fluffy Bum. Fluffy Bum was hand selected as a baby bunny by the E.B.P. (Easter Bunny Pickers) as a choice Easter Bunny candidate.

His name described him perfectly. All the other little bunnies were very jealous of his perfect "FLUFFY BUM".

OFFICIAL
EASTER BUNNY
ACADEMY

Over time, Fluffy Bum grew up and was one day
ready to head to The Official Easter Bunny Academy.
His first year was off to a great start!

He started out with perfect grades in many subjects (Egg Hiding 101, Hop Away and Hide, Quiet on Delivery and Basket Decorating). He even got extra points for the Appear Fluffy and Cute class, which he mastered.

EGG Hiding
101

Basket Decorating

Hop Away &
Hide

However, there was one
little problem...

It all started one regretful evening, when Fluffy Bum got a taste for the chocolate he was putting in the different eggs.
Mmmm! Milk chocolate, white chocolate cream, even some rare eggs with the delightful gooey candy yolks in the center. Sooooo delicious!!
He couldn't get enough of it!

He was continuously caught putting candies in Easter eggs that had little Fluffy Bum bites taken out of them!

According to the E.B.P. this wasn't just a little problem. It was actually a very SERIOUS problem!

EASTER BUNNY
ACADEMY

Fluffy Bum wouldn't be able to advance to the final grade in The Official Easter Bunny Academy until he had gotten rid of this terrible habit! The other bunnies took notice that he was struggling with this habit and started to poke fun at him (VERY mean of them I know, but they were still very jealous of his perfectly fluffy bum).

Some of them would point and laugh and tease him.

This really hurt Fluffy Bum's feelings. He needed to find a solution to end his terrible habit once and for all.

He decided he needed to visit his great-great-grandbunny, Floppy Ears VI, to get some advice. Floppy Ears VI was the oldest and wisest bunny in town and also happened to be the most famous Easter Bunny the Academy had ever had!

So off he hopped,
in hopes of solving
his bunny woes.

Fluffy Bum arrived at his great-great-grandbunny's house and hopped over to him. Floppy Ears VI welcomed Fluffy Bum onto his lap.
"What is wrong, little Fluff Bum?"
Tears started to well up in Fluffy Bum's eyes.
"I have a terrible habit and I'm not sure what to do! I can't stop tasting the chocolates before I put them in the children's Easter eggs! I won't ever be able to become an Official Easter Bunny, like you, unless I can defeat this terrible habit of mine."

"Well Fluffy Bum, this is a problem for sure, but I will help you overcome this issue. I am glad you recognized you had a problem and came to me to ask for help. You see, no bunny is automatically just good at everything! We all have different things we struggle with, Fluff Bum, and it sounds like your biggest struggle is temptation. When I was a little bunny, I had a very hard time passing my Hop Away and Hide class."

"You see, my most famous trait, my perfectly floppy ears had created a perfectly annoying problem. Whenever I would try to quietly leave, my floppy ears would get caught up and stuck somewhere. I tripped over them a time or two and tumbled more times than I could count!"

"Really, Great-great-grandbunny?" Fluffy Bum asked. "I had no Idea that you struggled with ANYTHING. You were the best Easter Bunny our town had ever seen!"

"Of course I did, little Fluff Bum! Nobody is perfect and everyone has something that they struggle with. The important thing is that I found a solution to my problem!"

"How did you fix it grandbunny?"

"Well, I tried many different solutions but the one that finally worked was to tie my flop-ears back with carrot stems, so they were out of the way and I couldn't get tripped up by them."

"Oh wow! Can you help me beat my habit too?"

"Of course I can! Let's think about how to solve this
little problem you have. Why are the chocolates
so hard to resist?"

"The chocolates smell so wonderful! I catch a whiff of
them blowing in the breeze and my nose starts sniffing
and my whiskers start twitching and
it's all downhill from there!"

"I see! That is quite the challenge. To solve my problem, I tied my ears up and back with carrot stems. Can you think of something similar you could do to keep yourself from smelling the yummy chocolate?"

"Hmmmm," Fluffy Bum pondered. "I've got it! What if I plug my nose?"

"That is a great idea," Floppy Ears replied. "I think I know just the place to get a nose-plugger too!"

Off they hopped to a house that was close-by
with a clothesline drying fresh laundry in the
breeze. Nearby in the fresh grass, sat a little basket
full of extra clothespins.

Fluffy Bum hopped over in delight and plugged his
nose with one of the clothespins to test it out!
"This will work perfectly," he said.

"Wait," said his grandbunny. "You have figured out one step in fighting your habit, but I have another piece of advice for you. When you struggle with temptation, and want something really badly, it helps to replace the bad habit with a good one. Why do you want to be an Official Easter Bunny? Think hard about this," Floppy Ears said.

"I want to be an Easter Bunny so I can bring a smile to all the kids' faces!" Fluffy Bum replied.

"That's great! It's a wonderful feeling to make others happy, and that's what I love too! So how can we replace your bad habit with a good one?"

Hmmmmm. They both thought for a bit.

"I know Grandbunny! Instead of having a bite of chocolate I can focus on putting an extra little gift inside their egg, like a sticker or a fun toy!"

"That's it! You have discovered another step to help you beat your habit! I think there is just one more step to come up with to help you combat your problem and set yourself up for Easter Bunny success!"

"What else do I need to do?"

"It would be a good idea to fill your tummy up with something delicious before you deliver the Easter eggs. Can you think of another food you really like that would help you to be full ahead of time so you aren't as tempted by the chocolate?" grandbunny asked.

"I know! I LOVE carrots!" said Fluffy Bum.

"Yes!!! That is perfect, so before filling the eggs and delivering them, come to my garden and gobble up as many carrots as you can, so your belly is full and you won't be so tempted."

"Ok! I can do that for sure," Fluffy Bum replied, licking his little bunny lips as he thought about the yummy carrots.

VEGETABLE GARDEN

"Ok, you are all set now! You have figured out a plan. I know you can do this! Tomorrow, before heading to the Academy make sure to complete all 3 of these steps. I know you will pass your final exam and become an even better Easter Bunny than I was!"

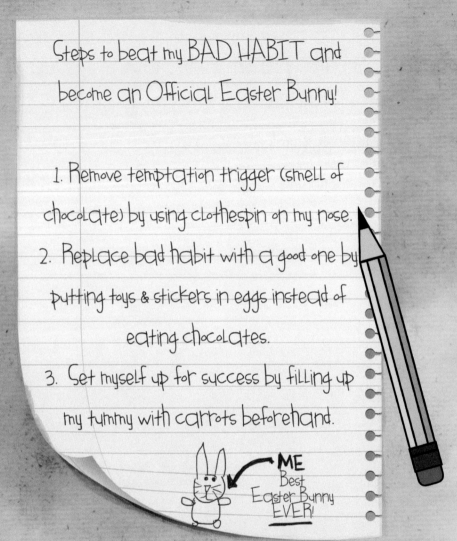

"Thank you so much for your help!" said Fluffy Bum while hugging his great-great-grandbunny. He hopped off towards his house to write all the steps down, so he would be sure to remember them.

The next day, Fluffy Bum took out the clothespin and pinched his nose with it. He grabbed his bag of stickers and toys and traveled to the carrot patch...

VEGETABLE GARDEN

where he munched and munched and munched!

When his tummy was satisfied, he bounded off to school, feeling proud and ready to pass his final exam!

During his test, the E.B.P. was blown away by Fluffy Bum's accomplishments! Not only was he able to complete each task, but he had also started a new tradition of adding little toys and stickers to the children's eggs! He passed his test and made Easter Bunny history with his new additions to the eggs! Fluffy Bum and Floppy Ears VI had never been more proud.

But just to be safe...
Make sure to leave some carrots out for him the
night before Easter to help ensure that temptation is gone
and your chocolates arrive uneaten and in one piece!

ABOUT THE AUTHOR

Carli Valentine is a children's book author and illustrator. She has authored and illustrated books including Cutest Pumpkin in the Patch, Turkey Trot, Christmas Is A Feeling, Big Plans for Tomorrow and Extra Special Heart. She resides with her husband, Keaton and 2 boys (Finnegan and Lochlan) in Ogden, Utah. When she's not sketching or scribbling down ideas for her children's books she likes to hang out with her family and volunteer at her son's elementary school and dedicates her time to various children's heart defect charities.

MORE BOOKS BY CARLI VALENTINE:

Tips for Combating a Bad Habit

1. Recognize that you have a bad habit so you can begin the steps needed to fix it. Without this step, Fluffy Bum would have never worked on his habit in the first place or been able to pass his test to become an Official Easter Bunny.

2. Try to understand why you are developing a bad habit. Are you feeling anxious? Having big feelings? Having trouble with self-control? Do you need more attention? Think about how you feel right before you engage in the bad habit. In the story, Fluffy Bum realized he was struggling with self-control and temptation.

3. Replace a bad habit with a good one. In the story, Fluffy Bum replaced his bad habit of eating all the chocolates with a good habit of putting toys and stickers in the eggs instead.

4. Try to catch yourself when you feel you are being triggered and feeling tempted by your bad habit. When this occurs try to focus on something else or keep yourself busy with an activity of some sort. Fluffy Bum filled his tummy up with carrots (his favorite) to help rid his temptation.

5. Give yourself grace. Getting rid of a bad habit is hard. If you mess up and fall back into a bad habit, try again to get back on track. The most important thing is continued improvement! Floppy Ears tells Fluffy Bum that it's normal to have struggles and problems and the most important thing is to keep at it!

6. Believe in yourself and praise yourself for working hard on defeating your bad habit. Recognize that you are trying hard. Be proud of yourself! You can do this! Remember the end of the story? Fluffy Bum was so proud of himself for working hard and as a result, is living his dream!

Made in the USA
Las Vegas, NV
09 March 2024

86939410R00024